What Happens Next?
DEALING WITH LIFE CHANGES

What Happens When I Have a Chronic Illness?

Emiliya King

PowerKiDS press.

Published in 2026 by The Rosen Publishing Group, Inc.
2544 Clinton Street, Buffalo, NY 14224

Copyright © 2026 by The Rosen Publishing Group, Inc.

First Edition

All rights reserved. No part of this book may be reproduced in any form without permission in writing from the publisher, except by a reviewer.

Editor: Caitlin McAneney
Book Design: Leslie Taylor

Photo Credits: Cover Ground Picture/Shutterstock.com; p. 5 fizkes/Shutterstock.com; p. 7 Lopolo/Shutterstock.com; p. 9 Andrey_Popov/Shutterstock.com; p. 11 Krakenimages.com/Shutterstock.com; p. 13 sunday pictures/Shutterstock.com; p. 15 Pixel-Shot/Shutterstock.com; p. 17 Studio Romantic/Shutterstock.com; p. 19 Yuganov Konstantin/Shutterstock.com; p. 21 Robert Kneschke/Shutterstock.com.

Cataloging-in-Publication Data
Names: King, Emiliya.
Title: What happens when I have a chronic illness? / Emiliya King.
Description: Buffalo, NY : PowerKids Press, 2026. | Series: What happens next? dealing with life changes| Includes glossary and index.
Identifiers: ISBN 9781499452549 (pbk.) | ISBN 9781499452556 (library bound) | ISBN 9781499452563 (ebook)
Subjects: LCSH: Chronic diseases–Juvenile literature. | Chronically ill–Juvenile literature.
Classification: LCC RC108.K46 2026 | DDC 616'.044–dc23

Manufactured in the United States of America

Some of the images in this book illustrate individuals who are models. The depictions do not imply actual situations or events.

CPSIA Compliance Information: Batch #CSPK26. For Further Information contact Rosen Publishing at 1-800-237-9932.

CONTENTS

What Is Chronic Illness? 4
All About Asthma 6
Dealing with Diabetes 8
A Gut Reaction 10
Blood Disorders 12
Chronic Pain 14
Your Support Team 16
Asking for Help 18
What *Can* I Do? 20
Glossary 22
For More Information 23
Index 24

What Is Chronic Illness?

Everyone has gotten a **temporary** illness before, such as the flu or a cold. However, some people struggle with **chronic** illness. These illnesses last months or years. Some last a lifetime.

If you have a chronic illness, you are not alone. In fact, 10 million to 20 million kids and teens in the United States have at least one, such as **epilepsy** or asthma. Knowing more about your chronic illness and the things you can do to feel better can help you **cope**.

Your Point of View

Autoimmune diseases are often chronic. With these disorders, the immune system attacks parts of the body instead of protecting them.

Dealing with a chronic illness may make it hard to focus, or pay attention.

All About Asthma

A common chronic illness in children is asthma. This **condition** makes it hard to breathe due to **inflammation** in the airways. During an asthma attack or flare-up, airways may narrow, fill with **mucus**, and keep air from getting through.

If you have asthma, you can keep away from asthma **triggers**, such as pets, dust, and pollen. You can take medicines, which are often taken in an inhaler. This tool creates a medicine-filled mist to help you breathe. You may need to carry an inhaler with you wherever you go.

Exercise can be good for asthma! When your lungs get stronger, they work better, and that helps you breathe easier.

inhaler

Your Point of View

You may still be able to run, play, and do sports even if you have asthma! Your doctor and care team can come up with a plan to **manage** your asthma.

Dealing with Diabetes

Diabetes is another chronic illness. This disease, or illness, involves how the body uses a sugar called glucose. Bodies need something called insulin to help the glucose pass into cells. That *should* give you energy.

People with diabetes don't have the insulin they need—or it doesn't work correctly. Blood sugar levels get out of control—and a person can get really sick. But there are ways to manage this illness. People with diabetes should take insulin medicine, eat well, and move their bodies.

Your teachers and school nurse can help you by allowing you to check blood sugar, take medicine, or have snacks when you need them.

Your Point of View

People with diabetes need to check their blood sugar levels often. This can often be done at home with a quick finger prick.

A Gut Reaction

Your digestive system helps your body get the nutrients and energy you need from food. Some digestive disorders cause pain and discomfort in the **gut**, or trouble going to the bathroom.

Kids with celiac disease can't eat gluten. The gluten causes their **immune system** to harm an important part of the digestive system—the small intestine. Then, it can't take in nutrients from food. If you have a digestive disorder, you will need to stay away from foods that trigger it. Luckily, grocery stores have many options!

Your Point of View

Gluten is a protein that's in grains such as wheat and rye. It's in many foods, such as breads, crackers, and baked goods.

Instead of wheat bread, a person with celiac disease can get gluten-free bread.

Blood Disorders

Blood has a very important job in the body. It carries oxygen, cells, and other necessary products where they need to go. Sometimes there aren't enough of one kind of blood cell, or they aren't working properly. Chronic blood disorders include anemia, which is a problem with red blood cells. Anemia can make you feel tired or weak.

First, you need to understand your blood disorder. People with anemia may need more iron. People with hemophilia need to be careful not to get hurt.

Blood makes up about 9 percent of your body weight!

Your Point of View

Hemophilia is a chronic disorder in which a person's blood doesn't clot, or stick together well. That means they'll keep bleeding longer than a normal person.

Chronic Pain

Some kids deal with pain disorders. They may feel pain in one part of the body, or in the body as a whole. The pain may come and go, or it may happen all the time. This can make it hard for kids to focus on school or enjoy play.

Kids who deal with chronic pain may need to have many tests to figure out what's going on. If there's an injury or illness that can be treated, the pain may go away with time. Otherwise, doctors will try to manage the pain with medicine and **physical therapy**.

Some people with chronic illnesses need to use wheelchairs, leg braces, or walkers. This helps them get where they need to go, without supporting the full weight of their body.

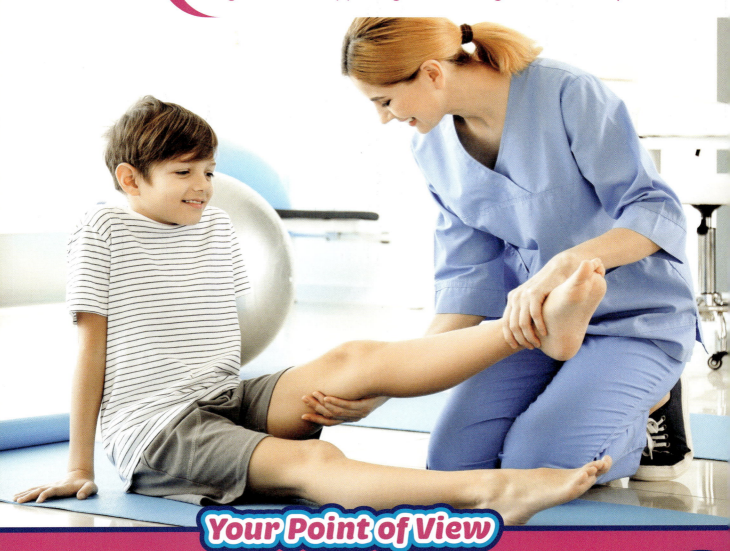

Your Point of View

Arthritis involves inflammation in the joints, or the places where bones meet in the body. This can cause you to feel stiff or achy.

Your Support Team

Dealing with a chronic illness may seem unfair. You may look at other people living their lives and feel upset. You may also feel alone.

It's important to know that you are not alone, however. You can lean on your support team—your parents or caregivers, doctors, therapists, and friends. Tell the truth about how your body feels. Then, they can find the right medicine, treatment, or therapy for you. It's also important to tell the truth about the inner feelings you have, such as sadness or worry.

Your doctors want to help you. That's why it's important to tell them how you're feeling.

Your Point of View

Some kids find it helpful to go to support groups of other kids with the same chronic issues. It may help you to know how others cope with their condition.

Asking for Help

You may need a little extra help in school or sports if you have a chronic illness. Your parents or caregivers can talk to your teachers, coaches, and school nurse. They may allow you extra rest, snacks, or sick days.

In sports, you may need extra gear. For example, if you have asthma, you will keep an inhaler with you. If you have arthritis, you may need a knee or wrist brace. You'll need to listen to your body to know when it needs a break.

Your Point of View

Teachers can help you catch up on any schoolwork you might miss for doctor's appointments or hospital stays.

You know your body best. Talk to a parent or trusted adult if something doesn't feel right in your body.

19

What *Can* You Do?

When you have a chronic illness, it can feel like everything is off limits. However, it's important to focus on the things you *can* do, not the things you *can't* do.

For example, you may not be able to play contact sports like football or soccer, but you may have fun swimming. Pollen might bother your asthma, but you can play outside as long as you have your inhaler. Ask your support team what you can do to make your life your own.

Your Point of View

Some chronic illnesses are mental illnesses, such as strong, lasting feelings of sadness or worry. It's important to talk to your doctors about this too.

With the right treatments and medicines, you can stay active and have fun—just like everyone else.

Glossary

chronic: Continuing or occurring again and again.

condition: A negative state of health.

cope: To deal with something in a healthy way.

epilepsy: A disorder affecting the brain in which a person has seizures, which may cause them to shake, fall, or pass out suddenly.

gut: The digestive tract, especially the stomach and intestines.

immune system: The body system that protects the body from things that cause illness.

inflammation: A bodily response to injury or disease in which part of the body becomes warm, red, and swollen.

manage: To have control over something.

mucus: A slippery, sticky substance made by the body.

physical therapy: The treatment of a disease or an injury using physical methods, such as exercises.

temporary: Lasting for a limited time.

trigger: Something that sets off another thing.

For More Information

Books

Mather, Chris. *Asthma Attack*. Minneapolis, MN: Bearport Publishing, 2023.

Shea, Therese. *What Happens When I Have Diabetes?* Buffalo, NY: PowerKids Press, 2025.

Websites

Health Problems
kidshealth.org/en/kids/health-problems/
Check out this resource that details many different health problems, from asthma to celiac disease.

Publisher's note to educators and parents: Our editors have carefully reviewed these websites to ensure that they are suitable for students. Many websites change frequently, however, and we cannot guarantee that a site's future contents will continue to meet our high standards of quality and educational value. Be advised that students should be closely supervised whenever they access the internet.

Index

A
arthritis, 15, 18
asthma, 4, 6, 7, 18, 20
autoimmune diseases, 5

B
blood disorders, 12, 13

C
celiac disease, 10, 11

D
diabetes, 8, 9
digestive system, 10

E
epilepsy, 4
exercise, 7

I
inflammation, 6, 15
inhaler, 6, 7, 18, 20

M
medicines, 6, 8, 9, 14, 16
mental illnesses, 20

P
physical therapy, 14

S
school, 9, 14, 18
sports, 7, 18, 20
support team, 16, 20